Casting Through Life

Casting Through Life

Poems by

Mathew V. Spano

© 2025 Mathew V. Spano. All rights reserved.
This material may not be reproduced in any form, published,
reprinted, recorded, performed, broadcast,
rewritten, or redistributed without
the explicit permission of Mathew V. Spano.
All such actions are strictly prohibited by law.

Cover design by Shay Culligan
Cover image by Meum Mare
Author photo by Thomas Peterson

ISBN: 978-1-63980-789-5

Kelsay Books
502 South 1040 East, A-119
American Fork, Utah 84003
Kelsaybooks.com

for Stephanie, Julia, and Nicholas:
  my eternal love and thanks for one heck of a fishing trip

Acknowledgments

Thank you to the following publications, in which versions of these poems previously appeared:

Acorn: "katydids"
Baseball Haiku: The Best Haiku Ever Written About The Game: "late afternoon," "radio static," "the dark stadium," "alone," "a chill wind"
Broken Cord: An Anthology of Writing About Alzheimer's and Dementia: "snow erasing"
Cicada: "set for fireworks"
Dust of Summers: The Red Moon Anthology of Best English-Language Haiku: "spring cleaning"
Frogpond: "the child's cough," "thawed garden," "tropical fish tank," "the dark place," "summer solstice," "suburban autumn," "blossoms again," "caught his limit"
Hellgrammite: "spring rapids," "Good Friday," "tropical," "blood moon," "imagining," "snow erasing," "spring flood," "an angry sky," "opening day"
Imps: "tropical," "extra innings," "fun house"
The Los Angeles Times: "the dark stadium"
Modern Haiku: "spring flood," "spring dawn," "Memorial Day," "unruly," "scenic," "imagining old age," "extra innings," "chainsaw idling," "fun house," "alone," "Halloween," "tow truck's," "spring cleaning," "on a tiny planet"
The Piedmont Literary Review: "an angry sky rides"
The Poets of New Jersey: From Colonial to Contemporary: "unruly," "tropical," "scenic," "March wind"

Contents

Introduction	13
the child's cough	17
trout season	17
thawed garden	18
spring rapids	18
spring flood	19
fallen nest	19
spring dawn, soft rain	20
Good Friday dawn	20
Memorial Day	21
unruly bluebells	21
tropical fish tank	22
caps tossed	22
scenic overlook	23
the dark place	23
late afternoon	24
an angry sky rides	24
summer solstice	25
radio static	25
set for fireworks	26
imagining old age	26
first noble truth	27
mockingbird's cries	27
extra innings	28
chainsaw idling	28
katydids	29
fun house music	29
the dark stadium	30
pier lights dim	30
back to school	31
blood moon	31

it slipped through	32
alone	32
Halloween	33
suburban autumn	33
voting at dusk	34
lazy autumn current	34
frozen river	35
snow erasing	35
Christmas dawn	36
on the way home	36
New Year's Eve	37
winter wading	37
a chill wind	38
tow truck's flashing	38
barren river	39
snap-off…	39
March wind jumbles	40
empty creels	40
window frost	41
snowmelt trickling	41
remembrance tree	42
spring cleaning	42
opening day	43
blossoms again	43
calm surface	44
the fly settles	44
caught his limit	45
the boot prints end	45
on a tiny planet	46
Afterword: The Haiku Remedy	47

Introduction

I've been writing haiku for over thirty years now. How did I ever come to fall in love with these tiny poems? I'd have to say my passion for reading and writing them was kindled by three different sources: one was a life-altering course in Japanese literature in my Comparative Literature graduate program taught by a fantastic professor. What struck me about the poets to whom she introduced us was their insistence on trying to evoke in the reader the same (or a similar) experience as the one that inspired them to write the poem down in the first place. They weren't just interested in telling you about their experience or suggesting what it could mean or represent; they really wanted you to *feel* it just like they did. Like pebbles tossed into a pond generating waves of ripples, these tiny poems, when dropped into the "pool" of a reader's mind, radiated waves of associations, memories, sensory experiences, and the like. Just a few words on a page in a certain arrangement with the power to transport a reader to another time, place, experience—it was pure magic.

At around the same time, I came across some terrific books on haiku: *The Essential Haiku* (translations of Basho, Buson, & Issa by Robert Hass—still the best translations for my money); *The Haiku Handbook* by Bill Higginson & Penny Harter (the Bible on how to understand and write haiku); and *The Haiku Anthology* edited by Cor van den Heuvel, which featured a history of the best English language haiku from the Beats on. I recall finding these books in the Atlantic Book Shop in Cape May, and they positively radiated light from a high shelf, beckoning me.

The third source, also at that time, was the art of fly fishing, which an older math professor introduced me to and with whom I fished up and down the trout streams of central New Jersey for decades. The subtlety, precision, and concentration that accompany fly fishing resonated with my interest in haiku and Zen meditation. It came about naturally for me to try writing haiku about some of the moments on the stream when time stands still and you lose yourself in the sound of the current, the rhythm of stripping and mending the line, the dance of sunlight on the water, and the feel of the fish's nibbling on the fly on the other end of your line way out there in the depths somewhere. These are the "timeless moments," as Norman Maclean called them, or "spots of time" that Wordsworth described, and I've been blessed to have experienced them for myself on the trout stream.

From there, I started noticing such "haiku moments" away from the stream, in everyday life—especially around my kids. Kids experience haiku moments all the time, but to them it's no big deal because they're always completely immersed in the present moment, purely and wholly invested in what they're doing right now, without overthinking it or watching themselves critically and shutting down the whole experience. That's why Basho told his students, "To write great haiku, find a three-foot child." One time I recall observing some little kids in a library standing by a fish tank. They were more interested in the "Do Not Touch" sign than the vibrantly colored exotic fish darting around in the tank. I don't even think they could read yet, but they intuited that those letters and words held magic and power—in their shape, sound, meaning—and they were transfixed by them, losing themselves in them, ironically smearing their little fingerprints all over the sign!

Baseball, like fly fishing, also has such moments where everything seems to arise and coalesce at once to create an experience where time stops and nothing exists separately from what's around it—everything *inter-exists* for a fleeting instant . . . and then it's gone. Like the moment when a long fly ball hangs forever in the night above the stadium, and everyone and everything is mesmerized by it, becomes one with it, as it sails through the dark on its way to . . .

nobody knows. A game-winning home run, or just a "can of corn" for the center fielder—that doesn't matter. When it's suspended in time and space, along with the players, coaches, umpires, fans, vendors, moths—that's the moment when everything is one.

My passion for haiku has been one long quest to capture such a timeless moment in words—be it on the trout stream, with my kids, or at a ballgame—in a way that can evoke it and recreate it in the reader's mind. I fervently hope that when the following pebbles drop into your consciousness, they continually radiate waves of rippling in your mind pool.

the child's cough
cracking and loosening
spring thaw

trout season
the current reconciles
old friends

thawed garden
Buddha and Francis
lean on each other

spring rapids
father and son untangle
their fishing lines

spring flood
mixing all the watercolors
to make mud

fallen nest
threaded with blue ribbon
from the birth announcement

spring dawn, soft rain
from the baby's room
happy nonsense words

Good Friday dawn
the boy tries to release
the dying trout

Memorial Day
in the war jet's wake screams
of gulls and children

unruly bluebells
in a school bus chassis
rusting in a field

tropical fish tank
fingerprint smudges
on the "Do Not Touch" sign

caps tossed
mayflies rising
with new wings

scenic overlook
buttercups peek through the cracks
in the viewfinder's base

the dark place
where the mower couldn't reach—
the first firefly

late afternoon
the pitcher's curveball drops
into the shadows

an angry sky rides
the river's surface—from fierce
thunderheads, trout flash!

summer solstice
the sprinkler completes
another arc

radio static
somewhere in the muggy night
a ballgame

set for fireworks
a child's balloon fades
into the rising moon

imagining old age
in the river mist
the ghost of a heron

first noble truth
a hooked fish still pulling
on a snagged line

mockingbird's cries
minnows keep swimming
into the net

extra innings
the vendor sips
his own beer

chainsaw idling
from the treetops cicadas
resume their singing

katydids
and kids imitating
katydids

fun house music
the pretty vendor flashes
her tongue stud

the dark stadium
moths and fans disperse
into the night

pier lights dim
traffic sounds ebb
with the night surf

back to school
centerfold fades and wrinkles
on the riverbank

blood moon
drawing us together
the hush of the surf

it slipped through
the poor fisherman's net
the autumn moon

alone
in the autumn night
the home run ball

Halloween
boys aim their flashlights
at the rising moon

suburban autumn
colors bounce harmlessly off
the SUV's

voting at dusk
stepping away from neighbors
to own his shadow

lazy autumn current
letting the fly line
untangle itself

frozen river
his knotted fingers
slowly tying flies

snow erasing
the garden's features
teaching my dad to shave

Christmas dawn
where the trout would rise
snowflakes brush water

on the way home
retracing my footprints
waves come and go

New Year's Eve
voices from the rapids
near the empty bench

winter wading
a submerged issue
of *Time*

a chill wind
whistles through the bleachers
the locked equipment box

tow truck's flashing
snowflakes sticking to the doe's
frozen lashes

barren river
the fish I thought I'd catch
darting through my mind

snap-off…
fishing with no fly
no fisherman

March wind jumbles
snowflakes with cherry blossoms
a crow's unanswered call

empty creels
the old man plucks a rainbow
out of the ice

window frost
children making peepholes
one for each star

snowmelt trickling
down the gravestones—in between
an acorn takes root

remembrance tree
felled by lightning
still blooming

spring cleaning
the final notes
of an old music box

opening day
in the old angler's spot
a boy with the same laugh

blossoms again
finding myself replaced
in the anthology

calm surface
the lost lure winking
from the riverbed

the fly settles
untouched
the moon ripples

caught his limit
an angler watches
the sunrise

the boot prints end
the current flows on
into the deep woods

on a tiny planet
tiny poems on
tiny things

Afterword: The Haiku Remedy

If Auden dubbed the twentieth century "the age of anxiety," how would he diagnose the twenty-first? Recently, it occurred to me that it would be somehow appropriate to consult AI on this question. Its answer was chillingly accurate:

> If W.H. Auden famously called the twentieth century "the age of anxiety," a poet reflecting on the twenty-first century might choose a term like "the age of distraction" or "the age of disconnection." These descriptors capture the profound influence of digital technology, social media, and the fragmentation of attention and community that characterize our time. (ChatGPT)

Still, I found that the answer, like so many generated by AI, merely scratched the surface. To add a human perspective to AI's diagnosis of "the age of disconnection," I'd note that we are more than ever disconnected from our own bodies and senses as well as our experience of the natural world. Essentially, we've come to live with our heads in "the cloud"—i.e., the data cloud up there in the ether to which the mind seems increasingly connected and upon which it increasingly depends. Arguably, it wouldn't be too hyperbolic to assert that we have become addicted to screens and scrolling, cut off from the immediate situation and surroundings, in a kind of technological trance.

With the arrival of AI, we could also be well on our way to alienating ourselves from our own inner nature and imaginative powers. Now, we have AI to think for us, create for us, even generate experiences for us. Our fascination with the virtual world may be replacing our fascination with the natural one. A poster I saw once in a shopping mall several years ago seemed to predict this trend. It was an advertisement by an environmental organization that featured two images juxtaposed: one showed a child's hands holding a cellphone with an image of a frog; the other was virtually identical except the child's hands (wet and a little slimy) held an actual frog. Ironically, the poster was displayed on a mall kiosk just outside a busy cellphone store.

Add the Technological Revolution to the Industrial Revolution of Auden's day, and we arrive at our contemporary, postmodern lifestyle: fast-paced, hyper-competitive, profit-driven, consumerist, predatory, and yes—to use AI's terms—distracted, fragmented, and disconnected.

If history is any indicator, however, the pendulum may well swing back. After all, we can't escape nature: much as we might ignore her in our techno-trance, she will snap us out if it and demand our attention. Hopefully, we can begin to awaken from the trance ourselves before she has to do it for us, possibly in an abrupt and violent manner. As George Carlin once said referring to our alienation from, and abuse of, the Earth, coupled with our inflated call to action to "Save the Planet": "The *planet* will be just fine—the *humans* will be f—ed!" Our awakening, as has been the case throughout the history of our species, will hopefully begin with our artists—our medicine men and women, our shamans who, as C.G. Jung noted, so often begin the healing process of bringing us back to ourselves:

> Therein lies the social significance of art: It is constantly at work educating the spirit of the age, conjuring up the forms in which the age is more lacking . . . to compensate the inadequacy and one-sidedness of the present. The artist . . . brings it [their vision] into relation with conscious values, thereby transforming it until it can be accepted by the minds of his contemporaries according to their powers. (*Collected Works, Vol. 15*)

As inconsequential as it may appear, the humble haiku as an art form is uniquely positioned to address our postmodern "one-sidedness," and the haiku poets that have spread around the globe taking the Japanese art form to more languages and cultures than any other poetic genre may already have quietly begun the healing process.

If the shadow side of our postmodern globalization means a deregulation of health and environmental standards, a circumvention of labor laws, and an overall reduction of the powers of local governments to serve productivity and big business, then haiku would seem to pose an artistic challenge to these values. In the "haiku moment," the poet experiences an expanded present (counter to the business emphasis on "futures" and "stock projections"). The haiku poet identifies with nature, as opposed to the conquest of nature to meet market demands (consider the exploitation of the rainforests.) In the haiku moment, the poet experiences awakening in the unique confluence of local circumstances and in the transience of this moment (as opposed to valuing broad trends and continuous patterns to serve business ends—consider re-forestation, tree farms, and the like). Finally, haiku take us out of the dominant, utilitarian, automated perception of modern life, and would seem to have no "useful" end other than to reconnect us to nature as a home from which we have alienated ourselves.

Haiku, then, as a literary art form, can be just the medicine we need. It can serve as a small but powerful voice in a counter-hegemonic discourse against the shadow side of economic globalization, a protector of the local and the natural. It can remind us to remember our bodies, and "inter-be" (to borrow Thich Nhat Hanh's term) with nature and with one another. It can provide an alternative to the extremes of exceptionalism, consumerism, and aggressive hyper-competitiveness. It can help us to come down from "the cloud," *slow down,* and live more authentically. How often have we, as postmoderns, complained to one another that life is going by too fast, passing us by, as we sit like passive spectators at the car race that our own lives have become? Haiku can help us to live more like Thoreau, whose wish was ". . . to live deep and suck out all the marrow of life," or as Ryokan who, returning to his home which had just been cleaned out by a robber, wrote:

Left behind by the thief—
The moon
In the window.

(trans. John Stevens)

About the Author

Mathew Spano has fly-fished the small streams and rivers of central N.J. for the past forty years. In that time, his poems have been published in various literary journals, books, and anthologies—large and small. In addition to fly fishing, his scholarly work in completing his Ph.D. in Comparative Literature at Rutgers University also influenced his creative work, which has thus far culminated in two books of poems and short fiction: *Hellgrammite* (Blast Press, 2016) and *Imps* (Blast Press, 2018). He currently works to take what wisdom the river sends his way and apply it to his job as Chair of the English Dept. at Middlesex College in Edison, N.J. where he also teaches World Literature and English Composition.

www.ingramcontent.com/pod-product-compliance
Lightning Source LLC
Chambersburg PA
CBHW030916170426
43193CB00009BA/868